Page Turners

The Angels

Sue Leather and Julian Thomlinson

Series Editor: Rob Waring
Story Editor: Julian Thomlinson
Series Development Editor: Sue Leather

HEINLE
CENGAGE Learning

Australia • Brazil • Japan • Korea • Mexico • Singapore • Spain • United Kingdom • United States

HEINLE
CENGAGE Learning

Page Turners Reading Library

The Angels
Sue Leather and Julian Thomlinson

Publisher: Andrew Robinson

Executive Editor: Sean Bermingham

Associate Development Editor: Sarah Tan

Director of Global Marketing: Ian Martin

Content Project Manager: Tan Jin Hock

Senior Print Buyer: Mary Beth Hennebury

Layout Design and Illustrations: Redbean Design Pte Ltd

Cover Illustration: Eric Foenander

Photo Credits:
37 Jordan Tan/Shutterstock

Copyright © 2012 Heinle, Cengage Learning

ALL RIGHTS RESERVED. No part of this work covered by the copyright herein may be reproduced, transmitted, stored, or used in any form or by any means graphic, electronic, or mechanical, including but not limited to photocopying, recording, scanning, digitizing, taping, Web distribution, information networks, or information storage and retrieval systems, except as permitted under Section 107 or 108 of the 1976 United States Copyright Act, without the prior written permission of the publisher.

For permission to use material from this text or product, submit all requests online at **www.cengage.com/permissions**
Further permissions questions can be emailed to
permissionrequest@cengage.com

Library of Congress Control Number: 2011909967
ISBN-13: 978-1-4240-4640-9
ISBN-10: 1-4240-4640-8

Heinle
20 Channel Center Street
Boston, Massachusetts 02210
USA

Cengage Learning is a leading provider of customized learning solutions with office locations around the globe, including Singapore, the United Kingdom, Australia, Mexico, Brazil, and Japan. Locate your local office at:
international.cengage.com/region

Cengage Learning products are represented in Canada by Nelson Education, Ltd.

Visit Heinle online at **elt.heinle.com**

Visit our corporate website at
www.cengage.com

Printed in Brazil
Print number: 01   Year: 2023

Contents

People in the story 3
Chapter 1   Good-bye, Coach 4
Chapter 2   The new coach 9
Chapter 3   Changes 14
Chapter 4   Pizza 19
Chapter 5   The pyramid... 24
Chapter 6   Back on the bus 29

Review 35
Answer Key 36

Background Reading
Spotlight on... Cheerleading 37

Glossary 38

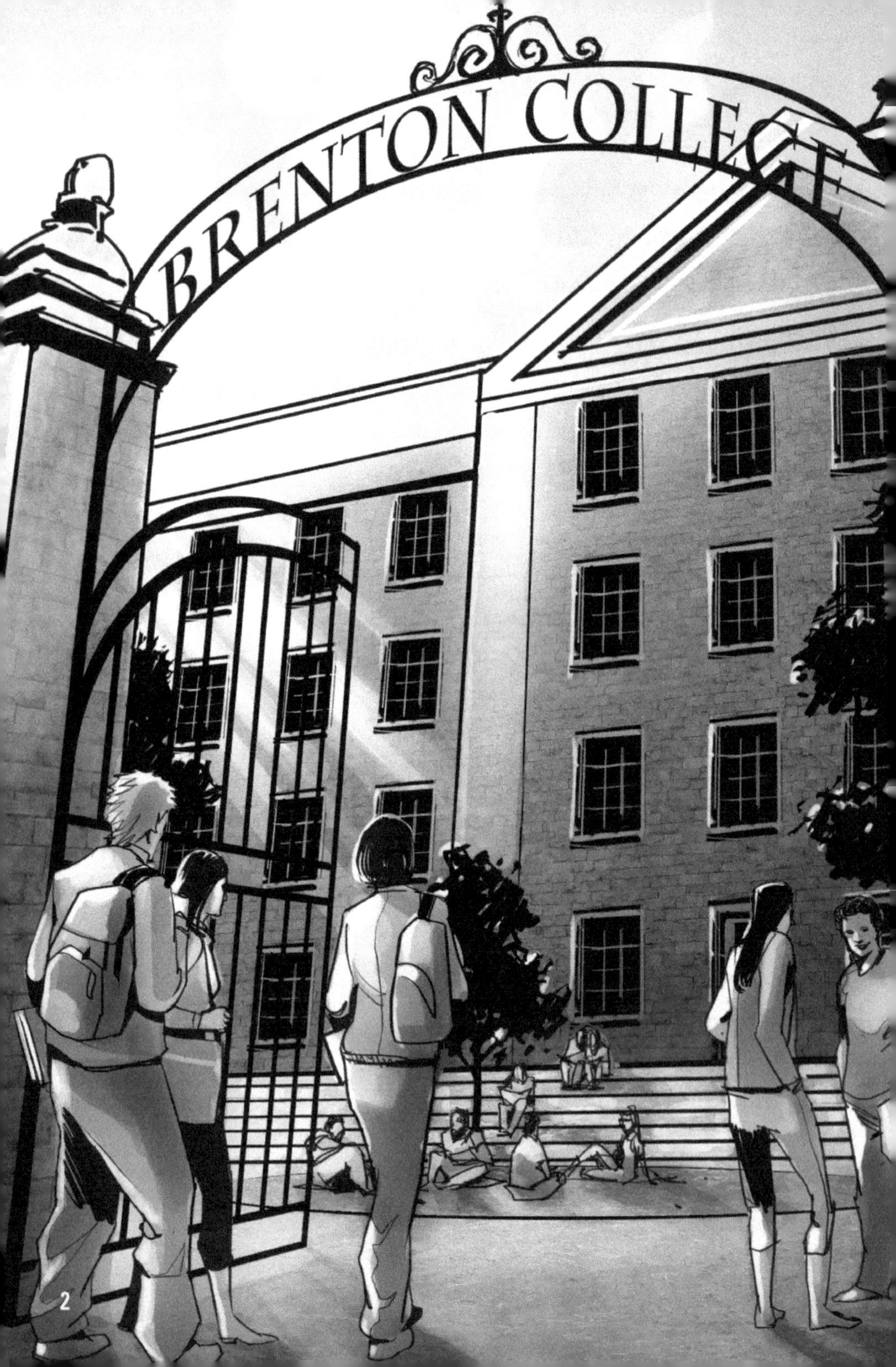
BRENTON COLLEGE

People in the story

Fleur Duval
Fleur is a member of
the Brenton Angels
cheerleaders, and
a communications student.

Ying-Chu Zhang
Ying-Chu is also a member
of the Brenton Angels, and
a business student. She is
friends with Fleur.

Belinda Garcia
Belinda is a member of
the Brenton Angels, and a
communications student.

Cindy Howell
Coach Howell manages
and coaches the
Brenton Angels.

Victor DeVeer
DeVeer is the vice president of
Brenton College.

This story is set in Brenton, a college town in the
northwestern United States.

Chapter 1

Good-bye, Coach

At last, we're home, Fleur thought, as the bus stopped outside Brenton College. This morning, she and the fourteen other girls in the Brenton Angels Cheerleaders, got up at 5 a.m. They drove for more than three hours on an old bus for a dance competition in the town of Salem.

The competition started late, and as usual, the girls did badly. They came in twelfth in the competition, twelfth out of thirteen. On the way back, their bus was late, and now it was nearly 10 o'clock, and they were all hungry. Fleur was tired and hungry and for the thousandth time, she asked herself why she was doing this.

"Hey everyone—don't worry, we're home!" her best friend Ying-Chu said to her, turning off the music player on her phone. Like Fleur, Ying-Chu did cheerleading and was one of the few really good dancers in the team. Nothing ever really made her unhappy.

"Don't you get tired of losing all the time?" Fleur asked her friend.

"You can't get upset about it, Fleur," said Ying-Chu.

Fleur didn't say anything to that. Ying-Chu was right, as usual. Coach Howell stood up at the front of the bus.

"Our great leader," said Fleur quietly, and Ying-Chu laughed.

"Girls," Coach Howell began, "before you all go home, I have something I want to say. First of all, again, good job tonight. You all did your best, and that's the most important thing."

"But . . . I have some news. It's hard for me to say this, and I wanted to wait until after the competition. I'm leaving next month and moving to Los Angeles."

"Whaaat?" said the girls together.

"Why?" Ying-Chu asked.

"It wasn't easy to decide. As you know, my husband is a doctor, and next month he starts a very good job there. I'd love to continue here, but I can't coach you from L.A.!"

Coach Howell looked like she wanted the girls to laugh, but they were all quiet, thinking about what she said.

Not easy to decide? thought Fleur. *It sounds to me like your husband decided anyway.*

"When are you going, Coach?" Jenny asked.

"My last day is the 12th of next month."

Just over three weeks, thought Fleur.

"So who's the new coach?" she asked.

6

"I only told the college about it last week," Coach Howell replied. "I'm sure they are looking for someone right now . . ."

Not at 10 p.m. on a Saturday night, Fleur thought.

All the girls started talking at the same time.

"What do you think?" Ying-Chu asked Fleur.

"The State Championships are on March 20th. That's twelve, no, eleven weeks from now."

"They'll find someone," Ying-Chu said.

"Will they?" replied Fleur.

"Hey," said Samantha, turning back to talk to them. "What do you think will happen?"

Ying-Chu and Fleur were the oldest girls on the team and team leaders, so the other girls always came to them for answers. But right now, they didn't have any.

"I don't know," said Fleur. "I need to think."

◇✕◇

Two hours later in Ben's Café, she was still thinking.

"I'm surprised you're unhappy about this," Ying-Chu was saying, as she finished her ice cream. "You're always saying how bad she is."

"Well, she is bad," Fleur replied.

"That's true. She's nice, though."

"Sure she is. Babies are nice, too, but you don't want a baby as your coach."

"I thought you didn't like babies much," she said.

"You know what I mean," Fleur replied. "Anyway, she's not important now. DeVeer's important."

Vice President DeVeer looked after all the money for the college's sports teams. DeVeer liked success, and the Brenton Angels were *not* successful. He liked success and he liked money, and Fleur thought this could be bad news for them.

"Do you think he'll stop giving the team money?" Ying-Chu asked.

"It's too late to find a coach this year, isn't it? Look what happened to Richardson College."

Richardson College had lost its cheerleading team a year before. Fleur didn't want that to happen at Brenton. Some of the other girls didn't really care, she knew, but Fleur and Ying-Chu were serious about dancing and cheerleading. They wanted to dance professionally after college. Stopping the cheerleading team was bad for them.

"I guess we just have to wait and see," said Ying-Chu.

Fleur didn't want to wait. *You can't get things by waiting for them*, she thought. All weekend, she thought about what to do, and on Sunday night she had an idea.

Chapter 2

The new coach

On Monday morning, Fleur and Ying-Chu went to DeVeer's office. They were waiting outside when the vice president arrived.

"Can I do something for you?" he asked them.

"We'd like to talk to you about the cheerleading team," said Fleur.

"Come in then," he replied.

Fleur began to follow him into the office.

"I'm not sure this is a good idea," Ying-Chu said.

"Too late now," said Fleur.

DeVeer put his coat over his chair, turned on his computer, and went to get a cup of coffee.

"So, I'm guessing this is about Coach Howell leaving, right?" he said.

"That's right," said Fleur.

"Well, as I'm sure she told you, nothing is decided. We're going to think about it over the next week or two."

"Sir, we have an idea for you to think about."

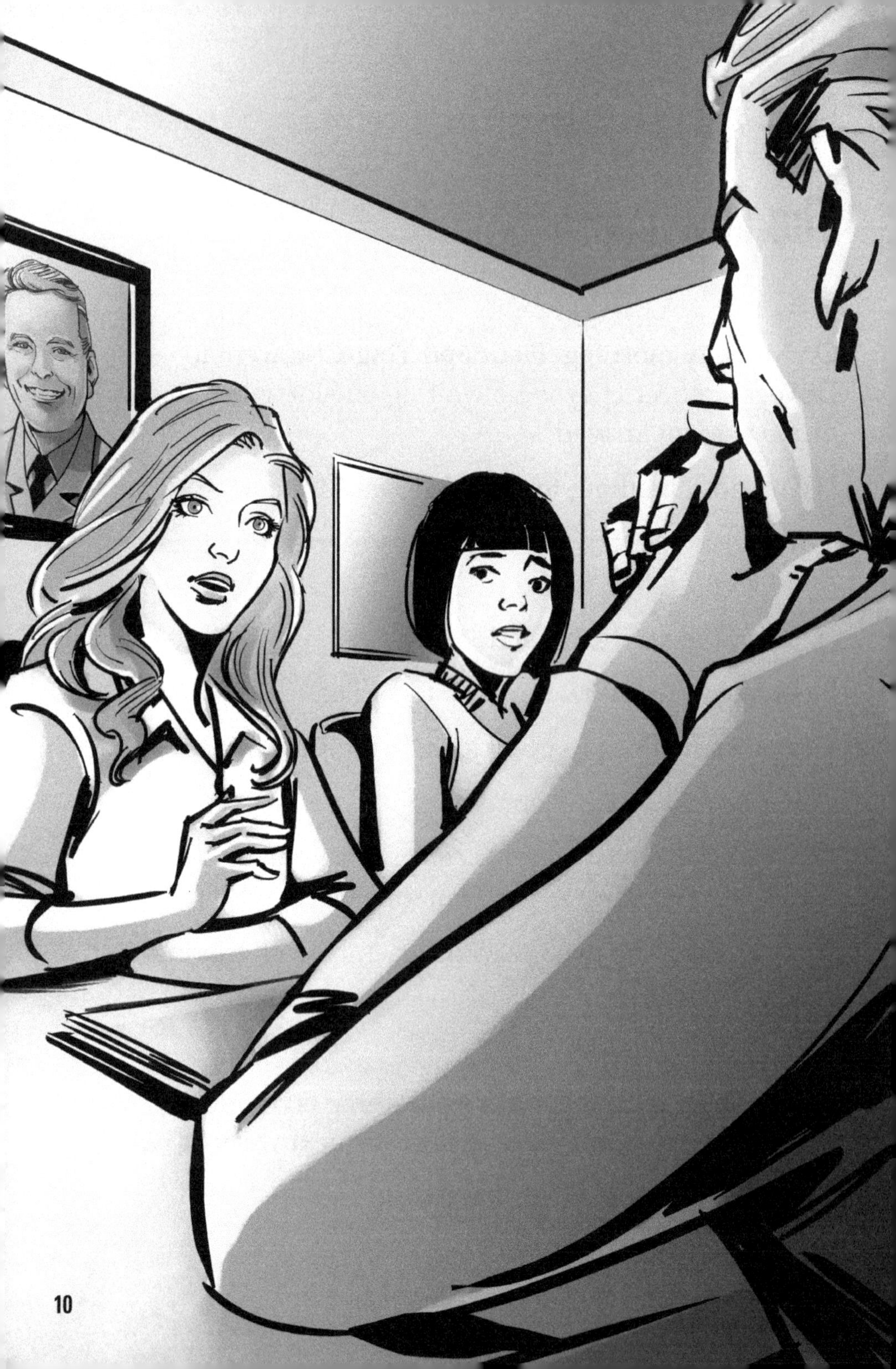

"You have?" DeVeer looked like he thought this was a little funny. "Let's hear it, then."

"We, that is, Ying-Chu and I, want to coach the team."

DeVeer looked surprised.

"Sorry, but you're students, aren't you?" DeVeer replied.

"We are, yes, but . . ."

"Listen," DeVeer went on, "I understand you're worried about Coach Howell leaving, but you don't need to worry. We . . ."

"No, sir, I'm not."

". . . are looking for a new . . . Not what?"

"I'm not worried," said Fleur. "Sir, the last competition we won was two years ago. Ying-Chu and I feel we can do better. We both did our tests to become assistant coaches and we're both studying to become full-time coaches. We can do this work part time, and it will cost a lot less than what you pay Coach Howell. Nobody knows the team better than we do. Most of all, nobody *cares* more than we do. We really want to start winning, and we think we know how to do that."

"And how *will* you do that?" DeVeer asked, looking at Fleur carefully.

Fleur took some papers out of her bag.

"It's all here," she said. "We need to look at every part of the team, the routines— the moves and jumps we do. We need to change our training, diet, uniforms, and hair. The makeup . . ."

DeVeer sat back in his chair, studying the papers.

"I can see you put a lot of time into this," he said. "I'll need to think about it. Give me a week or two . . ."

"Sir, it's only eleven weeks until the State Championships. We need to know . . ."

"Miss Duval, don't push me. I need time to think about this and talk to others about it. I'll be in touch, don't worry about that."

But they did worry. All the following week they worried about what DeVeer was going to say. Then on Friday afternoon DeVeer called Fleur and told her that she and Ying-Chu both had new jobs: coach and assistant coach of the Brenton Angels.

When the girls found out about their new coaches, they were surprised, and then they were excited. They all liked Fleur and Ying-Chu.

For the next two weeks, while they helped Coach Howell, Fleur put all her time into studying coaching. She was really worried before the first practice, but after they finished, everyone looked tired but happy.

"Really nice practice!" Jenny said at the end of the two hours. The others agreed.

"It was fun!" said Belinda.

"Different!" said Cameron.

"Thanks, Coach! Sorry, *Coaches!*" Hilary said. Everyone laughed.

But as the team left the gym, Fleur turned to Ying-Chu.

"That was OK," she said. "The girls did well. But we've got a long way to go, Ying-Chu. A long way."

Chapter 3

Changes

"That was good, girls," said Fleur after their routine at the football game between Brenton and Westway college. The girls smiled.

"But," Fleur went on, "if we want to do well at the State Championships, we're going to have to get much better. I have some ideas about that, which we can talk about at the next practice. So see you tomorrow. And no late nights!"

The girls all went to change. Only Ying-Chu stayed with Fleur.

"What did you mean—some ideas?" she asked.

"The first problem is the girls aren't very strong," Fleur replied, pushing back her hair. "We need a fitness plan."

"A fitness plan?" Ying-Chu replied.

"We're going to use this," Fleur told her.

Fleur showed Ying-Chu a book. On the front was a strong-looking man jumping up in the air. The book was called *Ultimate Fitness*.

"I see," Ying-Chu said.

"We need to look better, too," Fleur went on. "Better hair, better makeup."

Ying-Chu looked at her friend in surprise, but Fleur wasn't finished.

"Then there's the diet," she went on. "The girls aren't eating the right things at all. Pizza, ice cream, soda. It's no good. No good at all."

"Fleur, don't you think this is maybe too much?" Ying-Chu asked her. "I'm not sure the girls really want to work that hard. For them, cheerleading's just fun."

"How can we win anything if we don't work hard, Ying-Chu?" Fleur asked. "There's one more thing. We need much more practice. I asked DeVeer to give us two practices a day, and he agreed."

"Two practices a day!" Ying-Chu said. "The girls can't do that!"

"That's why we don't win," Fleur replied.

"I know you want us to win," said Ying-Chu. "I understand. Really I do. I know what it's been like for you at home . . ."

Fleur cut her off. The last thing she wanted to talk about was her troubles with her mother. "They just need strong leaders," she said, her face serious. "With a real leader—leaders, I mean—they can do so much more than they think they can. You can see that, can't you? We just need to push them."

◇◇◇

At the next practice, Fleur told the team about her new ideas. She talked to them about the diet, the makeup, and the new routines.

"Ying-Chu, give them the fitness plan, please," Fleur finished.

Ying-Chu gave out some paper.

"Fitness plan?" Belinda shouted.

"Practice twice a day!" said Cameron, reading the plan. "Morning practice at seven!"

"The competition's weeks away!" said Hilary.

"Yes, and we need to start getting ready now if we want to do well," said Fleur.

"No French fries?" Belinda shouted. "You can't be serious!"

◇◇◇

Over the next few weeks, Fleur really tried to push the team. But it seemed that as Fleur got more serious about her "fitness plan," the team got less serious.

One Friday, two weeks before the State Championships, the team was practicing. They were trying a new routine and it wasn't going very well. Fleur was getting red in the face, and the girls were looking at the clock.

"Come on!!" said Fleur. "Belinda, faster! We'll never win the State Championships running around like old women."

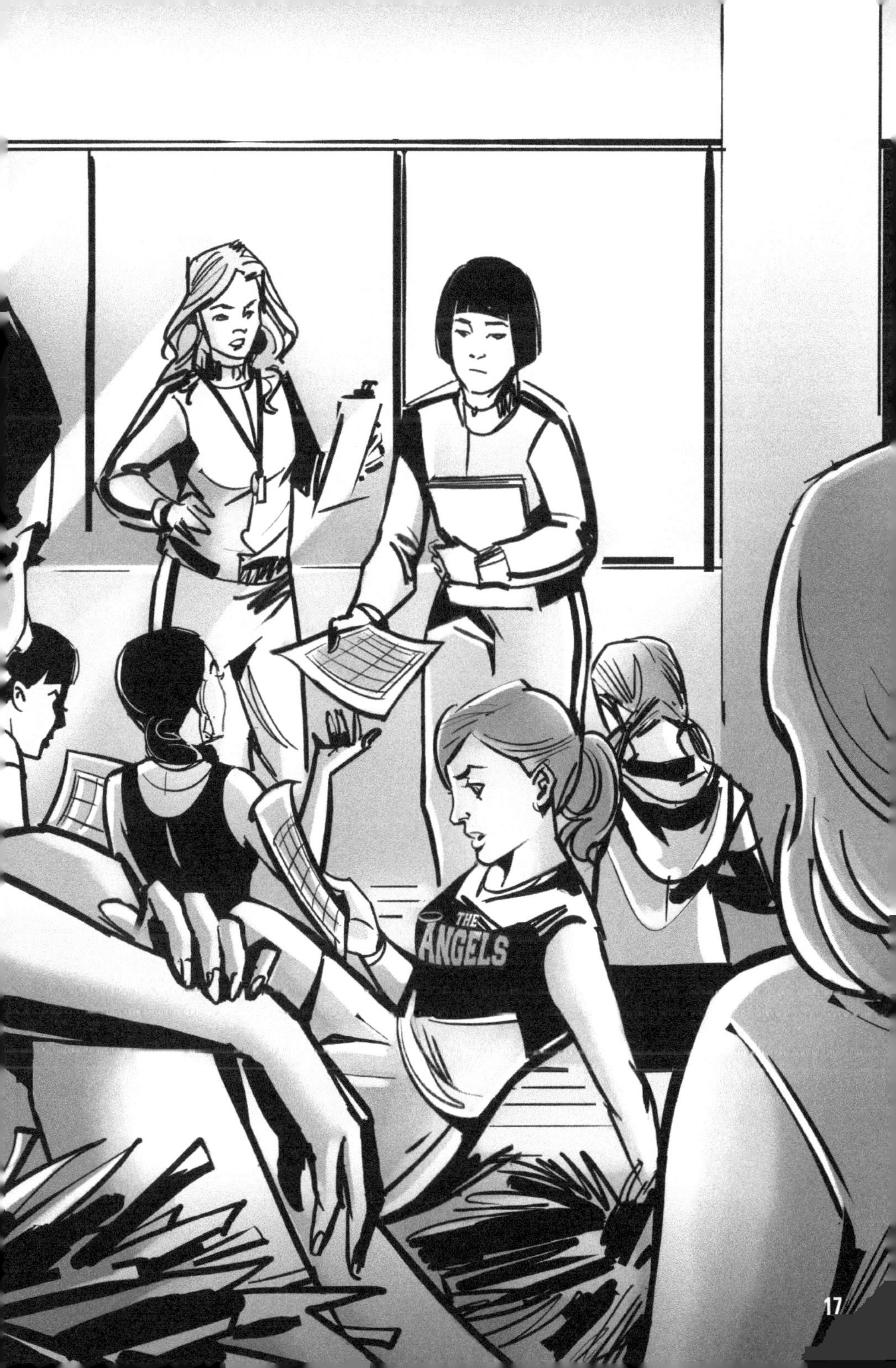
THE
ANGELS

As she spoke, her phone rang. It was her mother.

What does she want now? Fleur thought.

"OK," she said. "Ying-Chu, just keep them working. I'll be back in a minute." Fleur went out of the gym.

Ten minutes later, she came back. Her mother wanted her to do some shopping. As usual. Fleur tried not to think about it as she walked into the gym. *I can't think about her now,* she thought. *Only twenty minutes of practice left and we have a lot to do.*

But she couldn't do anything because nobody was there.

Chapter 4

Pizza

Fleur called Ying-Chu.

"Ying-Chu?" Fleur could hear laughing.

"Yes?"

"Where are you? Where *is* everyone?"

"We're at Ben's Café having pizza," said Ying-Chu.

When Fleur arrived, the girls were all sitting at a table, drinking sodas and laughing and joking. Three empty pizza boxes were on the table.

Those things must be 2,000 calories each, Fleur thought.

"Hey, Fleur!" Belinda shouted. "Pull up a chair. Let's get another pizza!"

"Not for me, thank you," Fleur said to the waiter.

"What can I get for you?" the waiter asked.

"Nothing, thank you," Fleur replied. "Ying-Chu, could I speak to you? Over here?"

"Sure," Ying-Chu said, and they went over to the window.

"Well?" Fleur asked.

"The girls were tired," Ying-Chu began. "They can't stay on the diet plan every day. They've been working hard and need a break. You too, Fleur. Won't you have a soda, at least?"

"No, thank you," Fleur replied.

"Fleur, you need to relax a little," Ying-Chu said.

"It's bad enough that you finished practice early," Fleur replied. "Did you do the new routines? No? I thought not. Finishing early is one thing. But pizza? Sodas? We've got a competition coming up soon. At least four of the girls are too heavy and here they are eating pizza."

"They're not too heavy," Ying-Chu said. "The girls are fine. Most of them. Anyway, it wasn't my idea to go for pizza. The girls all wanted it. It's not my job to say where we eat, is it?"

"Ying-Chu, that's where you are wrong. It *is* our job to say that. We are the coaches. We have to do what's best for the team. If you let people do what they want . . . do you think people *want* to train? Do you think they *want* to eat good, healthy food?"

"Let's get ice cream!" Belinda shouted, from across the room.

"See what I mean?" Fleur said.

21

"Listen, Fleur," Ying-Chu began. "Don't you think you're pushing the girls a little too hard? You have to trust them. They'll work hard if you let them."

"Trust them? Like I trusted you to finish the practice?"

"Well, not everyone is as serious about this as you, Fleur . . . as us, I mean. Some of the girls, well, I told you, it's just fun to them. They don't want it to become work, you know."

That's just the trouble, Fleur thought to herself. *They don't know that to win, you have to work. But I do. And I'm going to tell them.*

Fleur went back to the table.

"Girls," she began. Nobody seemed to be listening. This was no good. She had something important to say, and the others were going to listen. She pushed back her hair from her face. Thinking of something she saw on television, she picked up a glass and hit the side of it with her knife. Everyone turned round, looking surprised. *That's better,* Fleur thought.

"Girls," she began again.

Everyone looked at Fleur.

"You've done a good job so far," she began. "But this is just the start."

Someone laughed, but Fleur carried on.

"Winning is not easy, girls," she went on. "Think about any great person and think about what they did to get there. Do you think they became great by not working hard? By sitting around and not training? Venus and Serena Williams? Hillary Clinton? Do you think Hillary Clinton became great by eating pizza?"

"Was Hillary Clinton a cheerleader?" Belinda asked.

"That's not what I mean," shouted Fleur. "If you want to be good at something, you have to work for it! Do you want to do well in life? Or do you want to sit at home watching TV all day? Do you want to be winners or losers?"

Most of the girls were looking down at the floor.

"It wasn't like this with Coach Howell," Belinda said. Fleur wanted to get angry but she stopped herself.

"No, it wasn't," replied Fleur. "Is that what you want? Coming last in every competition? Being a loser all the time? Because if you do, please say so. If you girls all say, 'Fleur, I don't want to train, I don't want to be a winner,' then Ying-Chu and I will stop being coaches, and you can all do what you want."

Nobody spoke, so Fleur went on.

"I know you think we're too hard. But we're not doing this for ourselves. We're doing this for all of us. Girls, just trust me. Just trust me, from now until the State Championships. Will you do that, girls? Will you trust me?"

Slowly, the girls all agreed.

Chapter 5

The pyramid

For the next week, the Brenton Angels' training went better. The girls worked hard and tried to do what Fleur wanted. But it didn't last. As time went on, Fleur made them work harder and harder, and the girls started to slow down again.

"Be careful, Fleur," said Ying-Chu, who saw that trouble was coming. "You're pushing them too hard again. Some of them are ready to give up."

But Fleur just said, "It'll be OK, Ying-Chu. When we win the State Championships, they'll know why we're working so hard."

Just a few days before the Championships, the team was practicing their routine. They tried it two, three times, but Fleur wasn't happy.

"No!" she said. "It's all too slow. And the pyramid is just not right." The pyramid was the one of the most difficult parts of their routine. "Everyone has to move much faster. You too, Belinda." Belinda was the smallest girl, who went on top of the pyramid. "Let's do it one more time."

The girls groaned.

"Again?" they all asked.

"Yes, again."

Ying-Chu came close to Fleur and said in her ear, "Fleur, we need to rest. This is the fourth time now. The girls are tired."

"I know they're tired, but we have to get this right," Fleur replied. Then she turned to the team and said, "One more time, please. We need to get it right before we go."

The girls moved to get into the pyramid again. Everything went well at first. Then it was Fleur's turn to get onto the pyramid. Suddenly, the pyramid moved around a lot, and everyone thought that it was going to fall.

After a few seconds that seemed like an hour, the pyramid stopped moving. Fleur said, "It's OK, everyone. Now, come on, Belinda." Belinda started to climb. She climbed up to the first level, then the second, and then she fell off.

"Aagh!"

"Belinda!"

Fleur looked down when she heard Cameron's cry. Belinda was on the floor, and seemed to have a problem with her foot. Everyone got down from the pyramid.

"Come on, Belinda," said Fleur, walking toward her. "Stand up. Let's get moving."

"I can't," Belinda said. "I think my ankle is broken."

Ying-Chu went to her. "Can you move it?" she asked.

"No," said Belinda. "It hurts."

Belinda was the only girl small enough to go on top of the pyramid. *This is it*, Fleur thought, *we can't go to the State Championships. It's too late to bring in someone else. This is the end!* Suddenly she became very angry.

"What a stupid thing to do!" she shouted at Belinda.

"But . . ." started Belinda.

"But what?" Fleur said. "That was the most stupid thing ever." Fleur suddenly looked around and saw everyone was watching her, with a strange look on their faces. For the first time, she saw that Belinda was hurt.

"Fleur!" Ying-Chu said. "Are you crazy?"

"I . . ."

"Stop shouting at her," Ying-Chu went on. "It's not her fault she got hurt."

"Oh, no?" said Fleur. "Whose is it then?"

"It's yours," Ying-Chu replied.

"Let's go outside," Fleur said.

"No, Fleur," Ying-Chu replied. "The girls need to hear this."

"You listen to me," Fleur began.

27

"No, Fleur," Ying-Chu replied. "*You* listen to me. For weeks you've been pushing the girls, and they're doing their best. I told you not to push them too hard, but you did, and now Belinda's hurt. Do you understand, Fleur? She's hurt because of you."

Fleur didn't know what to say. Ying-Chu didn't usually talk like this.

"She's hurt, and what's more, you're shouting at her for being hurt. Fleur, do you think it's OK to do that? Because I don't. I don't think it's OK at all."

"I . . ." Fleur began. She stopped because she didn't know what to say. "I . . . I . . ."

"Yes, *I*. That's all you care about, Fleur. This isn't about the team, is it? It's just about Fleur. Well, here it is, Fleur. I've had enough of it. I'm finished. Or you're finished. Do you understand? You go, or I go."

"Ying-Chu, wait," Fleur said.

"I won't wait. I tried to tell you, but you didn't want to listen. Who will it be, Fleur? Me or you? Do you want to ask the girls?"

She didn't need to. All of them stood behind Ying-Chu, and all of them were looking at Fleur angrily.

Fleur ran out of the gym without looking back.

Chapter 6

Back on the bus

Fleur was on the bed in her mother's small apartment. Her mother was in the living room, watching TV as usual. Fleur could hear the noise through the wall. She looked around her bedroom with its old paint and thin brown curtains and felt bad. This was what she was trying to get away from, she thought, and now here she was back again.

"I knew it was going to end badly." It was her mother. She was standing at the door. It was nearly lunchtime, but her hair was a mess and she was still wearing her bedclothes.

Fleur didn't speak. Her mother sat down on the bed next to her and took her hand.

"Nothing good ever happens to people like us, girl," her mother said. "You must know that by now."

Fleur didn't answer.

"If you try and be something you're not," her mother went on, "life's always going to push you down. I told you that when you first went to college. People like us, we're always alone. Why didn't you just get a job, like . . ."

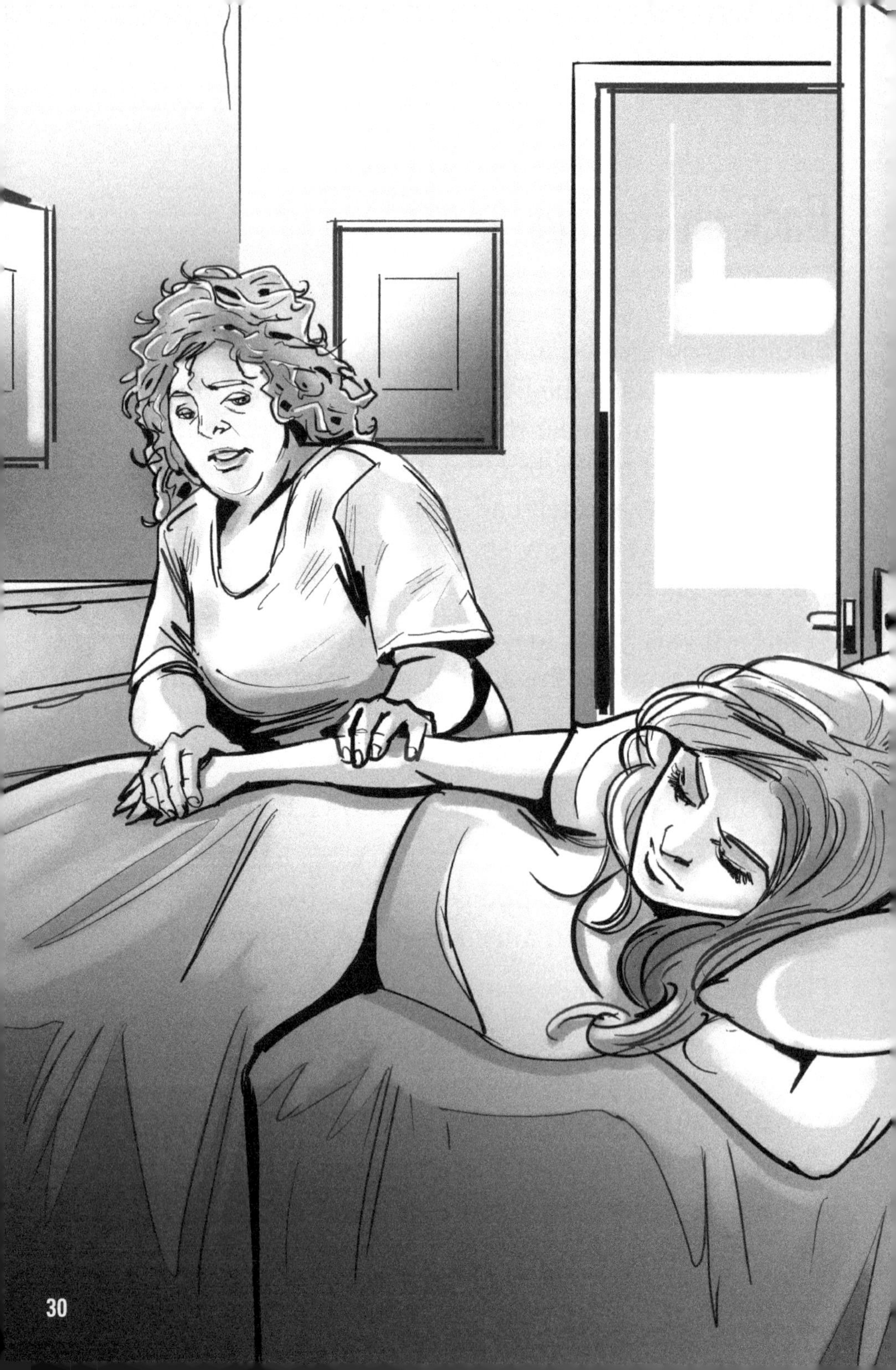

"Just go away, Mom," Fleur said.

Her mother turned and left the room, closing the door behind her.

People like us, her mother said. Was that true? Was Fleur really just like her mother? All her life she tried to be someone different, but here she was, in bed at lunchtime.

Ying-Chu was right, she thought, Ying-Chu was right. It is all about me. All about me trying to get out of here.

◇◇◇

The bus left for the State Championships at nine the next morning. When Fleur arrived at 8:45, the girls were there waiting for it, talking and laughing. They looked great standing there in their uniforms. It made Fleur feel good to see them. They looked happy. *They're happy all right*, she thought. *Happy without me.* Fleur wanted to turn and run then, but she put the voice out of her mind, and continued toward the bus.

The girls saw Fleur then and stopped talking. They looked at each other, as if they didn't know what to do. Ying-Chu turned and saw her friend, then came to meet her.

"Fleur," Ying-Chu said.

"Ying-Chu, I'm here to say sorry. I'm so, so sorry."

"Come here," Ying-Chu said, and put her arms round her. Fleur began to cry.

"Oh, Fleur," Ying-Chu said. Fleur didn't want to cry—there were things to say—but she couldn't stop herself.

"I just . . . I just wanted to . . ." Fleur said.

"I know, Fleur," Ying-Chu replied. "I know. I'm sorry as well."

They hugged for a few minutes, until Fleur stopped crying.

"I need to talk to the girls, don't I?" she said.

"Yes, you do," Ying-Chu replied.

"Do you think they will have me back? Will you?"

"Just talk to them," Ying-Chu said.

Fleur turned and walked over to the girls. They looked worried, not sure what was coming.

"I'm sorry . . . really sorry," said Fleur. "To you most of all, Belinda. What I said to you was wrong, really wrong."

Belinda didn't reply. Fleur went on in a quiet voice. "Ying-Chu was right. I was thinking all about myself. This is the only thing I was ever good at, and I just wanted to do well. I wanted to do well so much it made me crazy. It took Ying-Chu, and all of you, to make me see that. So, I'm sorry. But I want you to give me a second chance. Will you do this? Will you give me a second chance?"

33

The girls looked at each other, then at Belinda.

"Sure, Fleur," Belinda said. "And we're happy for what you did. You made us a much better team. We just need you to be a little less . . ."

"Crazy?" Fleur said.

"Yeah, crazy," Belinda replied.

The girls all laughed and hugged each other.

We're always alone, her mother said. *That was the problem,* she thought. *That's always been the problem.* But standing there with the girls, she didn't feel alone anymore, and that, at least, was a start.

Review

A. Match the characters in the story to their descriptions.

1. ____ Fleur Duvall
2. ____ Ying-Chu Zhang
3. ____ Belinda Garcia
4. ____ Cindy Howell
5. ____ Victor DeVeer

a. the smallest cheerleader on the team
b. the vice president of Brenton college
c. the new head coach of the team
d. the old coach of the team
e. the new assistant coach of the team

B. Choose the best answer for each question.

1. Why is Fleur so serious about cheerleading?
   a. She wants to be a professional dancer.
   b. She wants to coach the team after she graduates.
   c. Her mother wants her to be a good cheerleader.

2. Which of these is **NOT** a reason DeVeer agrees to let Fleur and Ying-Chu coach?
   a. The team can win more competitions.
   b. He gets to save money.
   c. He thinks cheerleading is a good sport.

3. Why does Fleur use the example of Hillary Clinton and the Williams sisters in Chapter 4?
   a. They are rich and famous.
   b. They are successful because they work hard.
   c. They go on diets and do not eat pizza.

4. Why is the real reason that Fleur wants to do well?
   a. She does not want to end up like her mother.
   b. She wants to be better than everyone else.
   c. She wants to take over the cheerleading team.

5. In the end, what does Fleur realize is the most important?
   a. friends
   b. doing well
   c. cheerleading

C. Are the following statements true (T) or false (F)?

1. The Brenton Angels won the State Championships last year.　　T / F
2. Fleur does not like to talk about her mother.　　T / F
3. Ying-Chu does not want the team to win the Championships.　　T / F
4. Belinda is the only girl who can go on top of the pyramid.　　T / F
5. Ying-Chu kicks Fleur out of the team.　　T / F
6. The girls forgive Fleur in the end.　　T / F

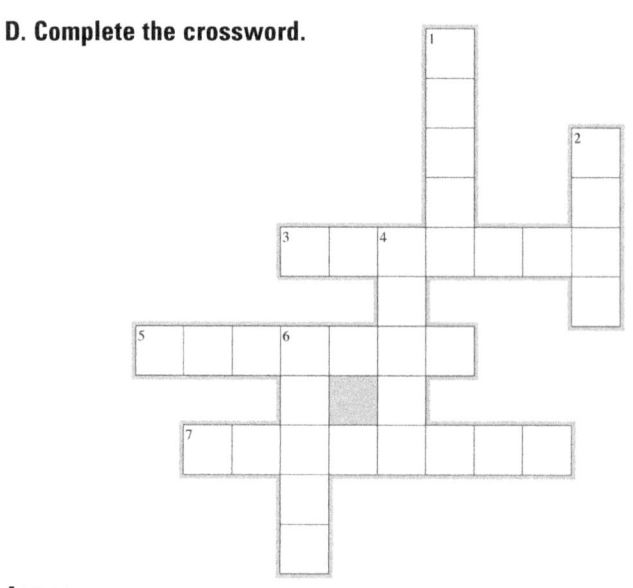

D. Complete the crossword.

Across
3. A(n) _____ is a set of dance steps which cheerleaders perform.
5. If you have _____, you do well at something.
7. When you _____ something, you do it many times to get better.

Down
1. If you _____ someone, you believe in or depend on the person.
2. When you go on a(n) _____, you eat less or healthier foods to lose weight.
4. When you are _____, you feel unhappy because something bad happened.
6. A(n) _____ is someone who leads and trains a team.

Answer Key
A: 1. c; 2. e; 3. a; 4. d; 5. b
B: 1. a; 2. c; 3. b; 4. a; 5. a
C: 1. F; 2. T; 3. F; 4. T; 5. F; 6. T
D: Across: 3. routine; 5. success; 7. practise; Down: 1. trust; 2. diet; 4. upset; 6. coach

36

Background Reading:
Spotlight on... *Cheerleading*

Cheerleaders traditionally support their school or college sports teams (like basketball, football, and baseball) during matches. The cheerleading team (or squad) cheer, dance, and do stunts (special moves which require skill and practice) to entertain people and get them to support the team, too.

All squad members wear the same uniform—usually a short skirt and a small top—which lets them move freely. They sometimes carry pom poms (colorful balls of cloth) in their hands and wave them around as they cheer. One of the most difficult routines, or moves, is the pyramid. In a pyramid, the cheerleaders stand on each other's shoulders sometimes three-people high.

A cheerleading squad in Singapore

Cheerleading is very popular in the United States. Over 1.5 million girls and women take part in this activity, compared to about 100,000 in the rest of the world. It has even become a sport of its own, and many teams take part in state or national competitions. Judges look at how well the cheerleaders dance and move with one another, their appearance, and whether their cheers are loud and clear. Teams also get extra points if their moves are unusual or creative.

Some people say cheerleading is not really a sport because teams win based on judges' personal opinions or views, rather than on objective things (facts) like scoring a goal. Cheerleaders say it is a sport because it is very physical and can be competitive.

> **Think About It**
>
> 1. Does your school have a cheerleading team? Would you like to start or join one?
> 2. Do you think cheerleading is a real sport? Why or why not?

Glossary

ankle (*n.*) Your ankle is between your foot and your leg.

climb (*v.*) When you climb a mountain, you go up it.

competition (*n.*) A competition is when two sports teams try to win a prize.

decide (*v.*) When you decide to do something, you plan to do it.

fitness (*adj.*) A fitness plan is a plan to make your body strong and fit by doing exercise.

gym (*n.*) A gym is a building where sports people practice their sports or exercise.

hug (*v.*) When you hug someone, you put your arms around them because you like them a lot.

hurt (*v.*) If your foot hurts it is painful and you can't walk on it.

practice (*v.*) When you practice something at sports you do it many times to get better at it.

pyramid (*n.*) In cheerleading, a pyramid is made when people stand on each other's shoulders.

routine (*n.*) In cheerleading, a routine is a short series of movements such as jumping or lifting your legs.

success (*n.*) If you have success, you do well at something.

trust (*v.*) If you trust someone, you believe and depend on him or her.

uniform (*n.*) A uniform is a special set of clothes all members of a team wear so they all look the same.

upset (*adj.*) If you are upset, you feel unhappy because something bad happened.